Posthumes

POSTHUMES

BRADFORD MORROW

CADMUS EDITIONS 1982

First published in 1982 by:
Cadmus Editions
Box 4725
Santa Barbara
California 93103

MORROW, Bradford.

LCN 81-6964-8
ISBN 0-932274-25-0 (trade edition)
ISBN 0-932274-26-9 (signed edition)

Albas / Evenings

Steamer's but a mackerel
in a star's piscary.

Burlesquer's song

After thirty years
    this steady nonsense

tends to abstract
    invertebrate joy

keen roseblossoms
    bore us each, as

now our bridled stageshows
    bow like dumb stars

toward that soil where
    dulled petals

soon enough
    rescind.

Beneath the friable moon

I've seen the disconsolate faces
of the bony dead, as they drift
in continuous circles around the tower
which rises above Jefferson Market.

Defiant and unreal, they watch
for the frozen fires which history has eaten,
        they crouch like marvelous bells
high in the unmusical perch
aloft the swelled cylinder of browned bricks
and pass a watchful emptied eye
over the populated plain of Manhattan island
where fires have burned before.

        Here the howl flies:
yet no one hears, above the cultured din
of a traffic of ceaseless, peerless human work,
here in "the city of the finalists"
where moves more motion than could ever fill
        a constellation's calendar,
the voiceless words of warning.

Now there is no further sign.
        The movement and the fire are gone:
the men are gone
        and the friable moon
looks down upon a lapsed scenario
where still the hollow,
        toothless smirk appears "within"
the carved air, where
watchtower sat, where in time
        the watchmen walked and sat.

Chrome alba

Dawn,
   we were awakened
          by a feverish
        breeze and a mask of derangement
tightly was fastened upon
    our tired faces,

and we arose to hear
          sounds of burning air,
      and saw the fossil boys beyond
the bedroom wall as they cast
     stones across a vast,

motionless, antedi-
         luvian body
    of stone in kind, and mercury:
you turned to me, love, and turned
    your chromium cheek.

Evening: matters

We stood under the box-elder
looked out on a low-lined bank
        of evening clouds

& you remarked with certitude
"the sky is beautiful tonight,
        as beautiful

as a painting by Manet, Monet?"
which pointed up, I sensed, an inter-
        esting problem.

On Boscovich's law that bodies can never actually come into contact

Beneath the dichotomous moon we lay
the half-light caught in the window-frame
as unsymbolic stars and planets
                    roll overhead,
our bodies a chaos,
your breath I breathe:
                              never the worse
for failing again to disprove
the law of Boscovich.

Just another evening esse

A golden angel strode
        in silence, with celerity
out from beneath the great elm, across
the front yard on to my porch.
        Its actual startling presence

burned at mind and memory
        as I lit into the past
looking for some precedent: unnamed, unpegged,
unfaced, untagged, unplaced
        it was (in any case) winged.

        The angel coolly exerted a brownish
                burnt-gold light, there in lampless predawn.
This was not, it seemed, a reflective
light, although the substantial
        limits of its form were blurred

as it moved across a human plane
        of twenty yards, out under
the breathing trees. Lucretius, *Urantia*, Fort,
Browne, Swift, St. John had none of them
        prepared me for this particular

introduction. Demonic? no,
        beneficent, then? not really.
My angel bore no message, asked no questions.
Inside the house I was quite
        excited, but sober

and somewhat diffident.
        For weeks thereafter I sat up late
trying somehow to will it back.
That such an ostensibly shattering
    mythical esse could drift

unpenned across this manned horizon
        sans explicative weight
or sense was beyond consideration.
This wild angel was nine feet tall!
    Nothing was gained, changed, imparted.

Lax alba at Quinnipiac

The property of firms and unseen men,
    variously squat
dull pink tanks inform the busy bay
       beside the freeway:

pink like that knuckle-headed eel
    we found tangled
last winter in grey beach rocks
      on the sound:

for you oil-laden, impudent, stately
    and solemn
tankers dock and unburden their frenzied
      petroleum,

while you and I, at dawn, are passed
    and quite superfluous
from the bridge that spans Quinnipiac
     where we stand, watch.

The Fire-Drill

"In its simplest form the fire-drill, as the apparatus has been appropriately named by Professor E.B. Tylor, consists of two sticks, the one furnished with a point and the other with a hole. The point of the one stick is inserted into the hole of the other, which is laid flat on the ground, while the operator holds the pointed stick upright in position and twirls it rapidly between his hands till the rubbing of the two sticks against each other produces sparks and at last a flame"—Sir James George Frazer, *The Golden Bough*, "The Magic Art and the Evolution of Kings," I, ii, 208.

I

In simplest form the fire-drill
consists unfierce of two sticks:
one is furnished with a point,
　　the other with a groove and hole.
According to Frazer, worship's thrown
up to the fire which these resolve
　　as fire perplexes both word and thought
　　　　even in its simplest form.

II

These sticks are fashioned
beyond the eye, beyond the cones and rods
of savage intellect,
    and fit like quoin at the angle of stress
    to bear the weight of the world's love.

These sticks are such that tip fits groove,
    the latter laid out long on the ground.
        And "ini" . . . male, or operator
holds the pointed rod upright
twirls it rapidly between his hands
till the rubbing produces sparks,
    and at last:
        a flame.

Thus the simplest form of the fire-drill
draws on mystery at the limit
of mystery's tensile power.

III

But in form which fools this form
the fire-drill fashions an empty room:

hardly done, when walls and doors
are burnt away. It is the darker form of love
that flows to the source of woe,
            this latter fire-drill. It is a fire
eyes of men are drawn to more, as less
of the simpler form of fire informs the ground.
It is a fire where flame precedes
            the holy twirl of fantastic charts.
It is the fire which frozen sparks
like diamonds stuck in grateful gardens
            distending beyond the faulty mist.

            This is the fire
of unglad victory.

IV

Gardens in flame across the blue hill
    fume and rove in parallel
grooves. Entire groves of perfumed eucalyptus
explode with elemental drama
    driving out shadows like light at noon.

    Only deep mystical bins,
    set in rows by ancient tribes, mar
our pride and strip us
    of all fantastical fun.
A darkened shard recovered from the ruin
    suggests the rift between grace
    and so-called sin.

V

A gleaming row of teeth are pulled from the char:
    someday they'll be assigned a name
      (based on dental records,
you see): Tereus, Cecil, Ludwig, Sam
    and so forth.

Advanced decay rules out the possibility
our friend ate well, or groomed,   .
    or died in someone's arms.
Ludwig's jaw is broken too.
    Gradually we begin to understand
      the signs of struggle.

VI

In the burning speech
which issues forth from the lips of drought,
yet the signs of fire
that once was here, but now
is gone, continue.
Here again the wordless whirr
of unthought perplexes that spark
where the fires, unflamed, reside.

And here is form,
the fire and the bride.

VII

Neither wavers, nor stands fast:
a familiar figure down an odd road,
            or, no:
    the road recedes, as the figure
of mystery stands fast?
                    Not historical,
uninvolved in the smashing seasons,
it is an odd frame to which we attach
        our deviant colloquy,
and a gutless node
        where we word what we do not know.

It is the figure of uncorruptible ennui
        that holds firm the center of all things,
        the coldest center of blue flame,
        and dark middle of the burning shaft.
The simple fire-drill.

Nett: nil

A salient and arid wind
      has blown all night. This morning
the stillness of disorder has settled
along the streets where like a lost thought
it wanders out to count what has fallen.

      Much has fallen
during the night. Everywhere
lay analogues of what went wrong
      between it and what it
has loved: torn boughs, twisted grating,
paper bits, bones and rags.

Some diligent student of a human
      promise that never rose
to meet the golden orb which fits
the passage from that which might
      to that which is,
might later catalogue this dead stuff:

      but uncharged clouds
    break overhead
where soon it stood in hottest innocence,
unable to figure this ritual litter.

Posthumes

> . . . dead . . .
>   ahead.

—*Frag. unattributed.*

Posthumes

Darius Milhaud, last of *les six*, advised
    me (his final day
in Paris, from his highly polished
                  black and chrome wheelchair,

gaunt, arthritic, worn angel under his
    uninsured Légers
the Germans had left behind) the most
                 delicious roasted

chicken that he ever ate was cooked up by
    Brancusi, in the
great corner kiln in his studio,
                 used concurrently

for warmth, melting metals, roasting fowl & fish.
    By the kiln, Milhaud
continued, were three Mademoiselle
                 Poganys, in three

media, that gazed with illimitable
    demure as sculptor
and composers horsed down the steaming
                 meal, and, he pointed

out, gesturing animatedly with the
    fingers which had scored
Le Boeuf sur le Toit, mercurial
                 Poulenc did dishes.

Hampton Hawes in the Alps

Milan fell back behind us
                damp into the alpine night
our train just an hour behind its printed schedule,
            not bad, considering
mail was burned in bonfires that year
            much of it postmarkt in an earlier lifetime.

A showering darkness berthed
at the high Swiss border, travelers then awakened
            by a solemn customs man whose manner
                    and fine-pressed uniform
marked an enviable order of style in life
            more so in the middle of night.

Off again into higher passes
half-asleep in the lightless crowded carriage
four engines tugged the long train,
                headed first to Amsterdam
then Helsinki after that,
            a breathless black outside the window
interrupted by lightening on the lakes
            soundless, soundless and a spectral white
the heavy wheels of the train
            clacking deep and confident polyrhythms
to punctuate a raw
and raucous solo by Hampton Hawes.

Upon looking into Ethel Waters' *La Vie en Blues*

      Days of rage, days
of nameless unleashed desire,
the days of unfettered horror defined
in the paradox
              of an older hope.
Days that cut across an erudition bound in the body:
Ethel, when is knowledge the measure

      of hope, just as
it inevitably bolsters rage?
"Je ne fus jamais qu'une sauvageonne":
thus Rousseauvian
              minutes converge in
the hour of new philosophies, set forth by chanteuses,
froglike auntie Toms on holiday.

Garibaldi posthume in Washington Sq.

Disconsolate, Garibaldi stood, stock still
the white fresh patina reglazed
      his personal green
from cap-a-pied the metal pose
            of a Garibaldi gone—

his caracul hat disproportionately
small, beneath, the cramped cold grimace
      all heroic statuary
assumes one hundred winters later:
            musing? not musing, of course,

but made to mime a musing look, faced westward
toward the chimerical horror
      which Washington Sq.
hosts nightly, daily hosts, the voices
           of the brawnless dead

filter up through plane-leaves, from baked brick, over
the bony untriumphant arch
      & lodge for this instant
in its bronzy ear, then are gone, un-
           interpreted, curled, borne, quashed.

Even paranoiacs

      Even paranoiacs
have enemies, uncle Delmore said
(an astral cloud
    of reason mussed his troubled pate that Cambridge day)

the world-wearied now
and then throw themselves out real windows
suddenly to
    merge with surprised streets, or fly off bridges hung high

enough to get the job
done. Once in a while yr worst fear's
your clearest claim
    to responsible observation: simpler dicta

      don't abound: example
runs to fact: consider the beaver,
that communal
    star, which castrates itself that pond order may pervade.

¶For discussion of self-castration among beavers see Sir Thomas Browne,
Pseudodoxia Epidemica, The Third Book: Of Divers Popular and
Received Tenets Concerning Animals. Chap. 18. *Of Molls* also applicable.

¶Possible footnote (rejected). "Blast all furry thoughts, the
Canadian beaver, submarine symbol of the slow unhappy subintelligentsias,"
Marshall McLuhan, *Counterblast.*

The unfitted passage

SYMMES'S HOLE. An imaginary opening in the crust of the earth at
both the north and the south poles, which, in the opinon of John Cleve
Symmes (1780-1829), led to the centre. According to the theory
propounded by Symmes, the earth is hollow, open at the poles, and
capable of being inhabited, and contains several concentric hollow
spheres. Symmes lectured and wrote in favor of this theory and, in
1823, formally petitioned Congress to fit out an expedition to test it.
Symmes died in poverty, but his son, Americus Vespucius, revived his
father's fantastic theory in 1876. Phyfe's *5000 Facts and Fancies*, 729.

Symmes blew in the backdoor of Washington
    that day, his mind afire
                    with deep business
his cheeks aflush with deep
    business, scale models in his luggage,
                a pigskin sleeve
with psychotic maps,
    figures at hand and his pockets
innocent of ready cash,
                        Symmes
was a cowboy who lobbied hard
    in the wrong rooms, at the wrong time
for the wrong thing.
Charming if unshaven, pungent, docile,
    snakeskin boots molting
                beneath the whitest cherrytrees,
boosting pencils from the press-room.

Black caverns at earth's end
   wait for Symmes to find them out.
Black caverns that wind
           to the center of the moving world
   wait for Symmes, where subterranean
kingdoms vie, populated by
vast, improbable concentric cities
        and darkening ware.

Money was not forthcoming
   for a cowboy to find the center of earth
of course, and models of ways
       were fed to bins
maps pawned off for the vellum.
Shortly thereafter, with cowboy wile,
   Symmes got as close to his particular
grail as a perfect vision
      of a passage
into the brightest center
   of the burgeoning world would allow.

Another posthume

A warm and muggy winter
along the darkening sound,
the foghorn has been blaring
across the stretch of water
for three days running.

     Three nights
I have sat in my room, now
the lamp spreads a yellow light
on the table and the ceiling
overhead, soon it will be time
to fry up calamari for dinner.

     And then I think of you
Thomas Browne, your strange
book, *Pseudodoxia Epidemica:*
the work of pure idiot savantry.

Your wife was a patient woman
as you came home from the wintry
channel, wet sand in your boots
on a night much like tonight,
with seven dead pelicans flung
over your shoulder in a bag.
Brought them bloody into the kitchen
in order to test your theory
about the direction and strength
of a hurricane which never came.
Seven pelicans hung upside down,
seven floppy beaks pointing every way.

My own kitchen, unlike yours
is dense with the dull smoke
of olive oil and fried squid.
Pelicans do not dangle overhead
as the set comes on and I watch
Marlon Brando as Christian Fletcher
in *Mutiny on the Bounty:*
    we all have, it would seem
our own unallied
and self-defining dream.

Curriculum

A politics of disavowal jars
the amber study of Picard, who
like some pterodactyl that grew
and lost its webbed wings
is ancient as the free speech
movement. A generation later,
after the dissolution
of two marriages in two countries
Picard pours perrier in the book-lined
room, under the warm and watchful
gaze of his eldest daughter.

Wall-eyed and unvirgin, Sal
frowns like a rastafarian madonna
as Picard shows me three of his
            most valued treasures:

on the left is Swift,
Mechanical Operation of the Spirit
wherein "the corruption of the senses
is the generation of the spirit"
and on the right we have de Broglie,
a prince and ever vernal,
whose dictum "each phenomenon
has an infinite number
of explanations, each of which
is equally valid" Picard
has always favored.

And between those two on the oaken
shelf sits a small quite famous
book, one that Sal finds most
accessible, *The Restaurants
of London* (1928) by Hooton-Smith.

Mr Belknap's use of deep imagery in business

The simplest agèd shit you could imagine
     reigns unwobblingly
in the image-ridden intellect
of Mr Belknap, extraordinaire (let

"shit" signify risen gods: see what I mean).
     When stuck in that gap
between what should and is, Belknap,
the wunderkind of possibilities,

turns like a brazen Baryshnikov to tried
     anecdotes, spiced with
comedy, bunk and scatology,
enough to cloud the sharpest and lucid,

pellucid of minds. And it always works! The
     deeper the image,
more broken the flustered syntax, the
richer in blood-cash our Belknap becomes.

Concomitants

for Kathy

Standing lax at your bedside
en la sala de recuperación,
    sodium pentathol

tilting the room, I held your
quiet hand & stared out the scrubbed window at
    the remarkably frail

traffic cop, who two floors down
construed a blurred blue pencil summonsing our
    motionless bright red car.

36

Mon oncle

My great-uncle, Silenus,
possessed of a Laurentian spirit
and an unmanageable mortgage

on a villa in a foggy seaside resort town
finally made the newspapers
by selling his gardner and our cousin, Sarah

to an Ethiopian gentleman with cash
and a private army deep in the heart
of Montecito, California.

Bisbane's flower

Bisbane had a lyrical manner
             about him, as graceful
         as the evening bat round the lamppost,

when he manouevered the ivory
             fettucine about
         the bright tines of his fork at Bardelli's

on O'Farrell, before the "flower"
             (as Pirandello called
         it in his tragedy) at the corner

of his mouth bloomed, choked all will, & sent
             him on an unreserved
         journey to the pinkest seas of Baja.

The history of it

Rushed into the burning middle
of its masturbatory decade before its vocabulary
        extended beyond ten grunts,

its doting progenitors could
quickly see their umpteenth male offspring
        would be a man in a hurry,

its vertical measure stuntd
at a tenderest age, applied itself therefore
        to numerological pursuits,

having amassed a small fortune
in genetics futures, its third marriage was
        addled by a battery of lawyers

whereafter it fled to a vernal
Mexican villa with a lanky male nurse,
        tended it after the specialists

had shrugged off, now kept within a rare
precolumbian urn behind the bar of the chicest
        faggot disco in Mazatlán

Passing from the Provinces

Anything that's got a head
may be beheaded.

Yr amanuensis

is troubled: they said
I failed
        by offering bad advice,

& too failed as I offered
no advice
        and my master erred
unaccustomedly,

and finally failed
when I showed
        my master (whose views
are crystalline & whose
affairs are in order)

the right path
wch he chose not to follow.

A spate of hysterical letters
consequently ensued.

        This is for the
birds, o my master.

To a friend in wake of a ballyhoo

for Kenneth Rexroth

I

Conjunction of much in a close room
              is bound to generate
fire, we knew:
        Herodotus the historian pursues
the griffin in his mediterranean heat,
its thorned wings winding heavy wind
              representing quickness,
tenacity lodged in its strong
        hooked snout,
attentively the griffin's ears are pricked:
        the symbol of guardianship.
Herodotus the historian has seen the living griffin
              though griffins are not.
Too, Aristotle at the fount drank deep
        came up in his cups,
and still believed the buzzard's
              got three balls.

Come, wax : gone, waned : all
        beneath the fumed clouds
and driving rain.

44

II

At the mirrored heart of your widest sorrow,
at the deepest bound of your deepest sorrow
        what is known and what propounded,
what is learned and what done:

before your graceful stock of other tongues
pulled like love to our single tongue,
            beyond whim of memory
begin with a boy
        running buckets of warm beer
up to the patrons of tired women
with bright bodies
in Chicago, before the crash.

Fugue of music, the fugue of mind
        followed you through a plain of grief
the fugue of sound marking the fugue
of mind, and the loss of love.

After the climbers, shoe-wets and chumps
        gunned one another down
in hotel rooms, and in foreign countries,
elsewhere full measure went with you.

        After one thousand fine works
of heart, you've traced a wide path
across the many generations.

III

A rolling multiplicity
                    of broken ad campaigns
troubles me nightly,
fresh concepts of buried youth,
                    native genius
and native strength slammed in the garbage
can trouble me nightly,
            five theorems without result,
                    as many bungled notions
        trouble me,
the words of friends & words of those
                    who loathe
trouble me nightly.

                    ("Never trust a bourgeois millionaire"
you told me at the bourgeois millionaire's.)
        You told me of the rise
of real evil in the world:
            transformation of surname into object
                    this is somewhere
close to the heart of evil.
        Many strong men gather
close to the heart of evil
        as its capacity and breadth
                    are perfect
        for the traffic it attracts.

Genetic dominoes tumble down, waves break
        without rhythm on the shore
                        their vortex soundless
and fully stayed,
        until the residue of fools
restores it & makes it act:

                        this you told me:
troubles me.

IV

            . . . sweetly ruin us
uncontentious
      making rich unseen
           clinging kin.

The law of inheritance . . .
      muddle of the mediocre foists

ennui's the source of

      . . . to fend off the simple things
like darkness, or boredom, or
the terror of death.

           Curriculum.

Euripedes slept in the folded robes
and never heard that tragic & comic
        are one.

V

Now the present scent of eucalpytus
fills the room in which we sit,
                    the room
you built.
            Many shade trees stretch
away from the window at your back
here in the library,
            several solid bars of light
have traveled from the sun's surface
                    to catch in your hair
and make you visible to my eyes.
                    For this
      I am grateful.

Many books and many years, many words
      and all this when the sorrow
and the joy are driven
                    into the inexplicable void,
      where perhaps we can finish
our dialogues in peace.

Aretini's kitchen

The passing knowledge of human nature . . .
is the birthright of every racketeer—
Bob Brown, *Gems.*

Like some bourgeois macbeth
I have studied you with ten devils behind yr eyes
and with lèvi-strauss exactitude done
all to mislay my memory, but you
require the white fires my terrible *compagnia* :
    to open your eyes
with a bicycle spoke, like they did
in the mountains of Karakoram last week.

    Andavam con li dieci demoni, the darkest
    horsemen begin to move
    away from the encampment and begin
    to storm & make signs.

Like some refugee from Aretini's kitchen
I have tried to dispel the possibility of you
yet clear acid poured into gelatinous pools
and the vision of your broken body
(all of it 'perfectly legal')
would not clear my head.
You have done everything to make me crazy

50

Passing from the provinces

Night in the form of mortmain
    broke itself in parts
posted several dead letters,

    did the rest
by telephone: then showed
    up unannounced,

laden with baggage & unpaid bills
    on the doorstoops
of all my friends, moved

    into the guest
rooms of a dozen houses where
soon it will be looked upon
    as a slightly
half-cocked cousin.

    By then I will
be packt & long
    gone.

This
first edition
of Posthumes *by*
Bradford Morrow, printed in
August of 1982 for Cadmus Editions,
consists of a trade edition and 150 numbered
copies. Cover drawing by Roland Ginzel. Num-
bered copies have been bound in boards and signed by
the author & the artist. Letterpress printing by
Grenfell Press; offset printing and binding
by Edwards Brothers. Designed by
Leslie Miller & set in Aldus,
Palatino, Weiss &
Weiss Initials.